THE BIOGRAPHY OF

KAMALA HARRIS

Ashley Stephens

TABLE OF CONTENTS

INTRODUCTION 1

CHAPTER 1: HER ORIGIN STORY 2

    Maya and Life Growing Up 3

    Lessons Learned and Stepkids 7

CHAPTER 2: RELATIONSHIP LIFE 9

CHAPTER 3: CAREER 16

    Degrees 18

    On Contemporary Issues 19

    Criticisms 21

    Political Ambitions 23

    Organizational Membership 24

    Previous Roles Held 25

CHAPTER 4: PERSONAL LIFE 27

    Music Tastes 28

    Hobbies 29

    Books 30

    Income 31

CHAPTER 5: OTHER KAMALA HARRIS FACTS TO REMEMBER 32

CONCLUSION 41

INTRODUCTION

The story of Senator Kamala Harris is one that begs to be told. When Diane Mariechild said that within a woman is the power to create, nurture, and transform, many minds must have turned to childbirth and pictured a mother building up her child. However, Kamala Harris continues to demonstrate that such a power goes well beyond the bond between a mother and her child. This book is a roadmap to a better understanding of a woman who has created a path for herself in uncharted territories, nurtured her dreams to fruition, and transformed the minds and lives of both friends and family as well as perfect strangers with her choices.

Kamala Harris is beloved by many for her fearlessly unrelenting will and patriotism. Her spirit, one she describes as 'joyful warrior,' continues to inspire people of all types to think of and fight for those who are less fortunate than they are, and to never back down in the face of prejudice and all other forms of oppression. More importantly, she teaches us to do this without anger or malice, but with love for our country at heart.

This book is a thorough yet succinct narrative on Senator Kamala Harris. It answers the question: "Who is Kamala Harris?" Enjoy.

CHAPTER 1

HER ORIGIN STORY

T hat Kamala grew up to be an academic and an activist is no surprise to anyone who has done even the slightest research on her background. Her mother, Shyamala Gopalan, had completed her B.S., M.S., and Ph.D. by the age of 25. This was the same year Kamala was born (Harris, 2019). This enviable academic success aside, Shyamala was also a naturally gifted singer—even winning an Indian national award for her vocal prowess. But the greater part of her later achievements was centered around medicine and activism. Most of her life's work in the field of medicine was focused on breast cancer research, and this led to some noteworthy contributions (Carson, 1985). Kamala's father, Donald Harris, was a Jamaican-American and a towering figure in the scene of academia in his own right.

He attended the University of California and, only three years after graduating, was given the title of professor by the University of Wisconsin. He would later go on to lecture and do some groundbreaking research at Stanford University for 26 years before retiring as an emeritus professor. With such high-achieving parents, it is no wonder Kamala and her sister, Maya, set the bar so far up that some might even consider it dangerously high.

Maya and Life Growing Up

Maya Lakshmi Harris West, like her sister, is a lawyer and a voice that refuses to be silenced even in the face of corruption and intimidation. She had the job of a political advisor to Hillary Clinton during the 2016 presidential campaigns. As an activist, Maya championed the cause for police reform. She was the principal author for a report on the issue entitled *Organized for Change: The Activist's Guide to Police Reform* (West, 2004). Strong as anyone who was raised by Shyamala Gopalan, Maya managed to complete her undergraduate and college education despite becoming a single mom at the age of 17 in 1984. Little is known about the father of Meenakshi Ashley Harris, Maya's daughter. Like Kamala, Meena was born on the 20th of October. Like her aunt, mother, and grandmother before her, Meena has bagged notable achievements for herself, both in her academics and in her career.

But do not picture a typical day in the Harris household when Kamala was a child as one cluttered with research papers and open textbooks strewn about the floor. Although Shyamala did not go on to pursue a musical career, her home was often one of melodies. This was supported by Donald Harris. Kamala recounts in her book, *The Truth We Hold*, her father's jazz collection and her mother's lovely voice as she sang to Aretha Franklin. One can, indeed, say that Kamala Harris's upbringing was filled warmth even as her parents set lofty standards for her and her sister.

Kamala Harris was born in Oakland, California. Growing up in a house that constantly hummed with music, she took an interest in the artform and joined a choir in a church she has described as 'black Baptist' (Harris, 2019). Even though Kamala's mother, Shyamala, had emigrated from Tamil in India years prior, the mother, scientist, and activist had not forgotten or abandoned her religion and culture. While Kamala and Maya were allowed to attend and sing at the black Baptist church, they also had an appreciation for their Indian roots and worshipped at a Hindu temple. By so doing, Kamala enjoyed growing up in a loving and harmonious family.

But things would change not long afterward. Shyamala and Donald had met in an unlikely situation. What brought the two lovebirds together was the fervent activism and protest that seemed to be a part of many U.S. campuses in the 1960s. They came to Berkeley to earn their doctorate degrees: Shyamala in nutrition and endocrinology, Donald in economics. The pair threw themselves fully into their studies, the protests, and debates. Although Shyamala was supposed to come back to Tamil and marry an Indian, she turned her back on that culture of fixed marriages and tied the knot with Donald instead. At the age of 25, Shyamala Gopalan had her Ph.D. in one hand and a newborn Kamala in the other.

One, as an outsider, cannot point the exact reason for the dissolution of the marriage between Donald and Shyamala Harris.

Kamala has stated often that she would rather discuss politics than talk about her personal life in public. Although her political ambitions and her recent decision to run for the office of President of The United States of America has demanded some personal information about her background, she and the rest of her family continue to reveal as little as possible. She does recall in her book, *The Truths We Hold*, the relationship between her parents getting colder with each day, regardless of the love they still held for each other. The earlier romantic whirlwind had long passed, and their incompatibility became more real with each disagreement.

Shyamala got divorced from Donald in 1971 and took on the responsibility of raising her daughters single-handedly. Even though Maya and Kamala got to see their dad on certain occasions like special holidays and during the summer, it was their mother who became the dominant parent figure in their formative years. Shyamala Gopalan made sure that her girls did not grow up with an inferiority complex. She fostered a pride for their African and Indian origins, and taught them to never be afraid. Kamala often remembers her telling her and Maya to make sure never to be the last to do anything, even though they "may be the first to do many things." Shyamala encouraged in her girls a sense of responsibility, not just in their own lives, but in service to others too. She described success to them as what one accomplishes in the lives of those around them.

She would often bring them to the lab with her, where they saw, firsthand, sexism and racism. Kamala still holds memories of her mother being discriminated against and passed over because of her race and accent. She writes, painfully, in her book about some of her mother's colleagues who thought Shyamala wasn't smart because of the Indian lilt when she spoke. The University also refused to make her a professor and chose a man who was decidedly less qualified instead. In all this, Shyamala exemplified all the values she taught her daughters. She was never one to look for pity when she had the power to influence the situation somehow, so she kept moving and working hard to achieve her goals. As Kamala describes in her book, one of those goals was to finally eradicate breast cancer while the other was successfully raising her daughters to be proud, productive, and upstanding members of society. She made great strides in the former and, as is evident today, achieved the latter.

After graduating from college and getting her J.D. (Juris Doctor) in 1989, Kamala was admitted to the bar in 1990 and began to practice as a Deputy District Attorney that same year. This was a dream come true for Kamala as she had hoped for a job in law enforcement. Many would remember her time as a prosecutor for the decisive role she played in protecting law-abiding citizens and putting criminals away. Her style, though thought by many to be aggressive, could also be seen as empathetic. As the San Francisco D.A., she created a platform where first-time drug offenders could be rehabilitated and afforded their high school diplomas or decent-paying jobs. This is opposed to the earlier status quo where such individuals were simply made to serve years of jail time. Nearing the end of Kamala's tenure as D.A. in 2006, there was an appreciable increase in the rate of convictions for felonies (52%

to 67%), and drug dealers (56% to 74%). More of her career achievements will be discussed in chapter 3 of this book.

Kamala's parents provided her and Maya with the necessary tools to succeed and thrive in a world that was most hostile to people of color and of the female gender. Shyamala and Donald did not set a path for their kids as some other learned parents might. They did not steer their children selfishly towards their own personal ambitions or in fulfillment of their own unrealized dreams. Instead, they strengthened their wings, taught them how to use the wind to their advantage, and left them to fly their own way. Although Kamala was too young at the time to have a vivid memory of it now, her mother would joke about a time when Kamala was asked what she wanted and replied, "fweedom." Kamala grew up listening to protest chants, debating voices, and Aretha Franklin.

Lessons Learned and Stepkids

Kamala Harris learned to be courageous from her parents who left their home country to live and study in America. Even though it was Shyamala's first time in the U.S., this did not prevent her from seeing the segregation and injustice that were prevalent in her new environment, or from doing something truly bold to stop it. Kamala learned from her mother how to be persistent regardless of pain, rejection and any other hurdle that might arise. Shyamala was hard at work on her thesis in pursuit of her Ph.D. right up until her water broke, and she was never hesitant to rebuke anyone who spoke in a manner that could be considered racist or insensitive. This she did, regardless of the position occupied by such an individual.

Kamala is married to a lawyer, Douglas Emhoff. She has two stepchildren who are Douglas's kids from a previous relationship. Contrary to what she feared, Cole and Ella, the stepkids, were not hostile towards her and chose to call her "Momala" instead of stepmom. In their opinion, the word "stepmother" has been vilified by Disney repeatedly and wouldn't be appropriate to use to address Kamala, who they care deeply about.

CHAPTER 2

RELATIONSHIP LIFE

Douglas Emhoff is the name of the man who captured the heart of Kamala Harris. And since then, all they have looked back on are memories of love and fun.

Douglas Emhoff was born in New York, just seven days before Kamala Harris was born, putting his birthday around the 13th of October. Talk about a match made in heaven. Another similarity he shares with Kamala is that he is a graduate of the University of Southern California's law school. The 54-year-old is said to describe himself humbly on his social media account as "a father, hubby, lawyer, and a wannabe golfer." Currently, he is a litigator and partner at DLA Piper Law Firm, where he puts in a lot of work for both their California and D.C. offices. So the bottom line is that he is doing practically well for himself and his family.

On family life, Douglas Emhoff has two children from a previous relationship — a son and a daughter. His son, Cole, is a graduate of Colorado College while his daughter, Ella, studies at Parsons School of

Design. Before Kamala Harris met his children, she was extremely nervous because she thought that they were not going to accept her. Kamala Harris acknowledged that she tried to look at things from their point of view because she had been in that situation before herself, when her parents had divorced. When Kamala Harris finally met them, she tried all she could to get them to be on the same page as her but according to her, she and Douglas Emhoff decided to take things slowly and not scare them or to push them away with the new presence that had just joined during a still-painful part of their lives. But fortunately for her, Douglas Emhoff's children were extremely understanding and very mature when it came to their dad getting married again. And just like that, Kamala Harris won her way into their hearts.

It is said that the two children get along very well with their new stepmother. They have such a good relationship that they even have a nickname for Kamala Harris. According to magazine reports, the two children refer to their stepmother as "Momala." They thought about it and came up with the conclusion that they should put the word "mom" and the word "Kamala" together and just like that, they picked a name that stuck with her. It turns out that Kamala did not have any children before her marriage with Douglas Emhoff. The two children Douglas has are from his previous relationship. But they are the proud parents of Douglas's two children, who are now a part of Kamala's family, as well. All this might sound like a fairy tale, but it is the true story of Kamala Harris's and Douglas Emhoff's relationship. She may also become the first female president of the United States, which would make her husband the first gentleman of the United States. These two have the potential to make groundbreaking history in the United States of America.

But the real question here is how did this dreamy relationship come about? Looking at both of them you would not imagine they would meet the way they did. You would probably think that they met in a fancy restaurant or a highbrow party, but they didn't. They met on a blind date that was set up by one of Kamala's close friends. It turns out that they thought that Kamala had been single for way too long and decided to get them together by setting up a blind date. This date worked in a way that was beneficial to both Kamala Harris and Douglas Emhoff.

It turns out that the date went better than either of them anticipated. They kept in touch for a while after the date before going on to date over the long term. News and reports from different magazines and articles carried the story of their love. The couple was extremely happy. They are said to have dated for about a year before getting engaged on March 27th, 2014. The engagement was said to be as low-key as possible. A thorough study of Douglas Emhoff would reveal that he is not one to waste time on throwing a big engagement party for himself and Kamala. He proposed to her in her California apartment by getting on one knee and presenting her with a diamond and platinum engagement ring. Yes, the kind of ring that is said to turn a lot of heads. Although the proposal itself very simple, it meant a lot to Kamala, so much that she said a very enthusiastic "yes." But come to think of it, why wouldn't she? The man in question shared a lot of her views, values and beliefs, and they were ready to stand by each other during all the hard times and easy times. The only thing left to do was to lock those values and vows between them in something as strong as concrete: marriage.

Kamala always said that she never believed in long-term engagements, so they went ahead and got married about four months after he popped the question. There was no point wasting more time delaying the inevitable. The heart wants what the heart wants. Their marriage ceremony was unlike any of the elites. Since the engagement was done quite discreetly, the wedding followed in the same manner. You might imagine that a couple of such influence would have an elaborate wedding with all the things the influential crowd typically likes to flaunt: taut dresses, flashy decorations, and every other thing that could elicit a "wow" reaction from people. However, the discreet couple chose instead to have a quiet, low-profile wedding arrangement. They were wedded at the Santa Barbara Courthouse. Following their legalized marriage, the couple broke a glass to commemorate the culture and beliefs of Douglass Emhoff, who is Jewish. According to different magazines, the couple would be celebrating their 5th wedding anniversary on the 22nd of August, 2019. How time flies, right? The two have been together for almost five years. Who would have thought that the blind date set up by Kamala's friend would bring forth a beautiful relationship that has been so successful? The couple has lived happily together since their marriage.

On previous anniversaries, Kamala Harris has been known to take to her social media profiles to wish a happy anniversary to the Douglas Emhoff, the man that makes her laugh. The sweet Senator Kamala Harris is a romantic like that who wastes no time in doing as much as possible to let her followers know how much her husband makes her smile. In one of her Instagram posts, on his birthday, Kamala Harris posted, "no one makes me smile as you do. Happy birthday to my incredible husband and favorite sous chef Doug! I love you." It turns out that Kamala Harris wanted to do something special for Douglas, and decided to begin with a well-thought-out post on her social media outlets showing how much she cares for her husband.

The reason why Kamala Harris referred to Douglas Emhoff as her favorite sous chef stems from the reason that Douglas loved helping her in the kitchen with cooking. And for one who loved to cook herself, Kamala Harris could not help but love having a partner in the kitchen. Cooking is a hobby Douglas Emhoff picked up after getting married to Kamala Harris, although he has several others, such as golfing and playing fantasy football. However, regardless of his other hobbies, Douglas Emhoff seems to enjoy cooking with his wife the most, and Kamala Harris seems to love his company in the kitchen just as much. The couple tries their best to spend as much time as they can with each other and their children. And what better way than cooking and dining to unite the family? Both Kamala Harris and Douglas Emhoff are busy people, so they try to make the most of the time they spend in each other's company. This is what has kept their relationship and family going stronger from year to year, unlike many other influential people who would suffer blows to their relationship and have fractured families as a result of their busy careers and tight schedules.

Another exciting thing about this couple is how they always rally round to show support to each other in everything that they do. They stand behind each other and make conscious efforts to be there for one another. This also contributes to strengthening the bonds they share even better.

In his own time, Douglas Emhoff also takes to social media as much as he can to flaunt his wife and all that she has accomplished. He talks about her book and creates awareness about her campaigns, and tries as much as he can to encourage her in everything she does. He is probably the strongest supporter of her presidential campaign, and this encouragement makes her want to go for the position even more. There's nothing more revitalizing than someone you love supporting you through all your decisions and all your endeavors. This couple has a way of making sure that the other has enough support to do anything that they feel passionate about and right now, Douglas Emhoff is doing a good job of it. He portrays his wife to the world in the way he already sees her. He is doing what he can to make sure that the campaign goes smoothly for his wife. He is showing that he could probably be a perfect first gentleman if the time finally comes, and that is what Kamala would need to preside over a country as extensive and bold as the United States. She would need support, a shoulder to lean on, a listening ear, and most importantly, a partner. No private assistant or advisor could possibly give Kamala Harris the support that someone as close to her as her husband would.

This power couple (as they are sometimes called) are philanthropists, known to have donated substantial amounts of money to different charity organizations. As of 2015, they both donated more than $30,000 dollars to various organizations, of which $10,000 of that money went to UNICEF. They try their best to help the less privileged. And there have been a lot of reports of them doing more. They earn a lot of money together, as well. As of 2015, the couple was said to have a combined income of $1.17 million, and they were not reluctant in making this disclosure. With all this said, it can be deduced that Kamala Harris and Douglas Emhoff are the kind of couple with a relationship based on support and trust for one another, no matter what.

This couple has gone through a lot together and have successfully pulled their way through it all to become the people they are today, which has made a lot of people think that Kamala Harris has the potential to be a serious title contender for the seat of the presidency if given the opportunity. From all the magazine articles that have been published about both of them since their marriage, these two are indeed a couple to watch out for.

CHAPTER 3

CAREER

Since bursting onto the political scene, Kamala Harris has occupied a good many offices, and borne many titles for her performance within and outside her area of expertise. Some of the accolades she has garnered range from awards and nominations to titles earned for commendable conduct in her sphere of influence.

Kamala Harris's rise to the limelight started off on a rather quiet note, but her decisiveness and tenacity were not to go unnoticed for too long. She got her first call to city politics in 1990. This was just slightly after her being called to the bar. And so, for a period of 8 years starting from 1990 up until 1998, Kamala Harris served and held the title of Deputy District Attorney in her native state of California in Alameda County. Soon after her eight-year spell as Deputy District Attorney, Kamala Harris moved on to hold the title of Chief of Community and Neighborhood Division in the state of San Francisco. In the year 2000, she received an invitation from the then-city attorney of San Francisco, Louise Renne, who arranged for Kamala to join her team.

Some four years after holding the title of Chief of Community and Neighborhood Division, 2004 to be precise, Kamala Harris was given upon the title "Woman of Power" by The National Urban League, owing to her commendable presence and actions in the political sphere. At the age of 40, Kamala Harris was fast gaining the attention of people in the political arena. So much so that she, who was asked to serve as chief of a division in San Francisco 4 years ago, rose to become District Attorney. For about a 7-year period ranging from 2004 to 2011, Kamala Harris held the title of District Attorney to the city of San Francisco. It's mind-blowing, really, how she grew through the ranks to such a high position in such a short while. But with determination, anything is possible — Kamala Harris proves that. A year later, when she turned 41 (2005), Kamala Harris added yet another title to her plethora. As a result of her influence in regulating black prosecution in the United States, she was awarded by The National Black Prosecutors Association with the Thurgood Marshall Award.

Kamala continued to reach for the stars, and after serving as San Francisco's District Attorney, she had a two-term tenure (8 years) as Attorney General to the state of California spanning from 2011 to 2017. During this time, Kamala Harris was recognized to be among the top one hundred most influential persons in the world. This recognition was revealed by *Time* magazine in the year 2013. Just how much cooler can Kamala Harris get!

After her time serving as Attorney General to California, Kamala Harris vied for the title of Senator. In a tightly contested election held in 2016 to succeed the then-outgoing Senator, Barbara Boxer, Kamala Harris emerged winner by beating her opponent with a whopping 62% of the votes. She thus earned the title of California Senator, which she still retains, from 2017 until the time of this writing. This election marked Kamala Harris as the third female United States Senator of the State of California. Following her rise to the title of Senator, Kamala Harris also holds the title of being named one of finest top one hundred lawyers in the state of California. This recognition was awarded her by *The Los Angeles Daily Journal.*

Degrees

Getting to this point in her life and career was no piece of cake, but Kamala Harris proved just why she is one of the very best in the business with the degrees she has backing her up. Her numerous degrees point to her well-rounded education and experience from different prestigious institutions of learning.

Kamala Harris's climb to the spotlight began with her first degree, which she bagged in 1989. She obtained her Juris Doctor (J.D.) from the prestigious University of California, Hastings College of the Law. From this point, Kamala Harris did not look back in her quest for enlightenment because some twenty-three years later, she added another degree to her collection. At the age of 48, on March 9th, 2012, audiences gathered to witness Kamala Harris being conferred upon the degree of Doctor Of Laws (LL.D.) by her alma mater, the prestigious Howard University at the District of Columbia. But even this massive leap onto the higher grounds of educational accomplishment didn't serve to satiate Kamala Harris's hunger for more honors. Three years later, when she turned 51, Kamala Harris added yet another degree to her plethora. This time, she was awarded the degree of Doctor of Humane Letters (D.H.L.) by the University of Southern California on May 15th, 2015.

Kamala Harris's climb up the educational ladder in terms of degrees did not end there either. Matter of factly, she went on to attain a consecutive Doctor of Humane Letters, (D.H.L.) almost two years later. But this time, the awarding institution was none other than her alma mater from which she got her Doctor of Laws (LL.D.) degree, Howard University. On May 13th, 2017, Kamala Harris got her fourth degree.

On Contemporary Issues

As of late, the United States has been plagued by diverse issues to which many different people have lent their voice and taken a stand. Sometimes, these stands are done in support or opposition of the decisions already made by the government in power in regard to the issue. Among the numerous amount of people who have spoken up to support or oppose these policies implemented by the government is Kamala Harris.

As a senator, one would expect she turn a blind eye to the decision-making process of the ruling government, but unlike other politicians, Kamala Harris has a feverish passion for her job, and hasn't lost her humanity in the process. This was proven by her stance against the bill against abortion already signed into law in some states. The bill regarding the abolishment or strict restriction of abortion has taken the United States by storm. Groups within and outside the country have aired their views, both in support and against the bill being signed into law. Kamala Harris was one of those who rose defiantly to condemn this bill proposing instead that states who wish to implement the new bill restricting abortion should come up with newer and improved policies regarding reproductive health that should be signed into law with the United States' Department of Justice.

Another hot issue which is still being debated in some parts of the world including the United States is the criminalization of sex work. On this issue, Kamala Harris is strongly against the criminalization of the trade and is of the opinion that such consensual behavior should not be criminalized since neither the sex workers nor their patronizers constitute any harm to themselves or the society. Moving on, the subject of guns which has long been debated, still remains a poignant issue in the United States and across the world. With public shootings getting to an all-time high in recent times, brows have been raised and tongues have wagged on whether or not to ban the importation of guns, pass stricter bills on the use of guns into law, and who should be given the blame for gun violence. Kamala Harris proposed that assault weapons in the AR-15-style category be banned. Knowing full well the ban on importation would only contribute a meager part, Harris went on to suggest that policies be made which allowed regular background checks to close loopholes, and that policies protecting gun manufacturers from being held responsible by victims be annulled.

In another key issue affecting the United States in terms of teachers' pay, Kamala Harris made an announcement in March of 2019 to increase the salary of the average teacher by $13,500. The estimated cost of this plan for a period of ten years would amount within the region of $315 billion. On other key issues like the Medicare for All bill of fellow senator, Bernie Sanders, and the Green New Deal; Kamala Harris is one of the many elites backing both bills to be passed into law.

Criticisms

With the right to critique comes the right to also be criticized. The current state of the United State leaves much to be desired in the eyes of both the elites and the lower classes, owing to the performance of the government on different levels. This has caused many people to react, and criticize the actions of the ruling government. However, it is important to note that criticisms do not necessarily imply that one is in the wrong. This is exactly the case with Kamala Harris.

It can be agreed that anyone caught in the spotlight is subject to the glare of onlookers. Kamala Harris has come under fire on some of her own actions, as well. As the Attorney General to the State of California, Kamala Harris was criticized for the way she handled things, particularly on account of the policies she signed into law and the cases she dealt with. The main point of these criticisms of her time in the office of the Attorney General stem from the belief that Kamala Harris's tenure was largely contradictory to the system in use — being unorthodox and parallel to the acknowledged system.

Another criticism to Kamala Harris comes from her stand on the subject of death penalties. Harris maintains the stand that death penalties should be suspended nationwide, even though she is herself a practitioner of the law. What her critics are still unable to wrap their heads around is the fact that during her time as Attorney General, she defended the death penalty sentence, but is totally against it on a personal level. Suffice it to say that her critics in this case haven't completely comprehended the distinction between work and personal life. It is Kamala Harris's job to defend the policies in the constitution, and is independent of whether or not she favors them.

Another point of criticism for Kamala Harris stems from her relative silence on the cause headed by the progressives for criminal justice reform. Critics find it unbelievable how Kamala Harris turned a blind eye to some cases of reforms, believing her to be biased in her stance on justice reforms in the country. Also, when voters approved the signing of the California Proposition 47 which helped reduce many felony sentences to misdemeanors, Kamala Harris took no stance in being for or against the notion. Her critics found this to be fishy, and they wasted no time in calling out the incident and Kamala Harris's perceived intentions in refusing to identify with the policy. And when it came to police shootings, another critical issue in the United States, Kamala Harris once opposed a bill which would have compelled her office to investigate and scrutinize police shootings.

This action elicited utter dislike from her critics, who wasted no time in smelling proverbial rats and drawing the attention of the masses to her actions, casting dubious glares at her intentions and reasons for taking such drastic actions.

Political Ambitions

As a woman whose political effects were seen by all within and outside her sphere of influence, it wasn't long before the idea was being bandied about that she could run for president in coming years. Since her time as District Attorney of the City and County of San Francisco in 2008, and her run up to the Senate in 2017, Kamala Harris has been touted for the position of presidency by friends and fans. What started off as a little hearsay developed into quiet rumors before finally blowing up into speculations that caught media attention, and Kamala Harris is quoted to not have ruled out the prospect when accosted by the media in June of 2018. From then on, Kamala Harris has been considered as a strong competitor to look out for, and the prospective flag bearer for the Democratic party in the 2020 presidential elections.

A month after being quoted by the media as not ruling out the prospect of joining the presidential race, Kamala Harris took to social media for advertisements and gained popularity. Reports reveal that she spent way higher than any other senator on Facebook ads. Still, in the month of July in 2018, Kamala Harris made the announcement of a prospective memoir she was set to publish. This move was interpreted as a growing interest from Kamala Harris to join the presidential race. Reports further reveal that Kamala Harris had been campaigning for candidates in different regions like South Carolina, Pennsylvania and Michigan.

When lots of attention had turned to Kamala Harris's activities, interpreting everything as an indication of her yearning for the presidency, she put an end to the speculations on the 21st of January, 2019. She made an official statement in which she was quoted saying she was a candidate for the 2020 presidential elections. Some 24 hours after going public with her candidacy in the general elections, Kamala Harris achieved a record for the most amount raised in one day after a candidacy announcement. The record tied with that set by fellow senator, Bernie Sanders in the year 2016. Albeit, Sanders soon overtook Kamala Harris again to maintain the title after going public as well with his desire to run for the 2020 presidential elections. Kamala Harris organized a formal campaign launch in her native town of Oakland, California on the 27th of January. The event, which was held at Frank Ogawa Plaza, welcomed over 20,000 people who came to show support to Kamala Harris's candidacy.

Organizational Membership

As a woman of value, a good team player, and a politician of great influence, it is no surprise that many people would want Kamala Harris to be on their team. For this reason, it is easy to understand why Kamala Harris is a member of many different bodies, organizations and caucuses.

She is currently a member of the Congressional Black Caucus owing to her influence on the black community in regulating prosecution in cases involving black people. Also, as a result of her Asian ancestry traceable from her mother who is of Indian roots, she is a member of the Congressional Asian Pacific American Caucus. A third caucus of which Kamala Harris is a member is the Congressional Caucus for Women's Issues.

Other bodies Kamala Harris is a member of include those related to work-specific committees. She is a member of the Committee on the Budget to the United States as well as the Committee on Homeland Security and Governmental Affairs of which she is a member of two subcommittees: the Subcommittee on Federal Spending Oversight and Emergency Management, and the Subcommittee on Regulatory Affairs and Federal Management. Another committee of which she is a member is the Select Committee on Intelligence which is comprised of carefully selected members. She is also a member of the Committee on the Judiciary to the United States. Within this committee, she is a member of the three subcommittees, which include the Subcommittee on Oversight, Agency Action, Federal Rights and Federal Courts; the Subcommittee on the Constitution, and the Subcommittee on Privacy, Technology and the Law. Her involvement in the Subcommittee on Privacy, Technology and the Law explains why she was involved in the prosecution against Facebook's infringement on the privacy of the data of its users.

Previous Roles Held

Kamala Harris has held many different roles since beginning her career after obtaining her first degree. These previous roles account for the many titles she has had over the course of her career.

She began as a member of the State Bar of California when she was called to the bar in 1990. She gradually rose to fame and soon took over the role of Deputy District Attorney in the same year she made the bar. She held the role for eight years in Alameda County, California. However, Kamala Harris was not satisfied with the role she held and she soon yearned to be involved in law enforcement. The quest to achieve her goals saw her take several positions on different state boards. Eventually, in 2000, Kamala Harris was recruited to San Francisco to serve as chief of the Community and Neighborhood Division. Three years down the line, she rose to the position of District Attorney of the City and County of San Francisco which she retained for two tenures. In 2008, she her desire to run for Attorney General to California. Two years down the line, she became the flag bearer of her party for the role by defeating fellow competitors Alberto Torrico and Chris Kelly for the role. She went on to defeat Steve Cooley, Los Angeles County District Attorney, to secure the role of Attorney General of the state of California. She retained the role for two terms following re-election in 2014.

While still in office, Kamala Harris expressed a desire to succeed Barbara Boxer as California Senator. On the 3rd of January, 2017, Kamala Harris was sworn into the office of Senator of California--a role she still holds to date.

CHAPTER 4

PERSONAL LIFE

Despite the fact that her political ambitions—especially her recent declaration to run for President of the United States of America—necessitate the revelation of some personal information, Kamala is still very careful about what she says concerning the happenings in her family and close friends. While some may be disappointed by this, it actually shows a level of discipline that is uncharacteristic of the average politician. But then, one cannot say, with all honesty, that Senator Kamala Harris is an average politician. Being the first to do many things (we'll discuss those things in a bit) and rising from obscurity to become a political figure that is well loved, respected, and even feared by those who have too much to hide, is not average by any measure.

Still, there *are* those things which we know about the beloved Senator.

Music Tastes

Growing up, Kamala was introduced to music of varying genres. Their home bopped, strummed, and vibrated with melodies from Bob Marley, The Jackson 5, Miles Davis, Aretha Franklin, John Coltrane, and many others. For an individual with such a diverse taste in music, it can be quite difficult to answer when asked about their favorite song or music artist.

This became a talking point on May 2nd, 2019, when she was asked the question live on CNN. Seeing as she had a long array of genres and musicians to pick from and not being able to come up with a quick answer, supporters of President Donald Trump were quick to paint this as an awkward struggle to a "softball question" (Conway, 2019). This was an unfair assessment of the situation, but almost anything seems to fly for some people when they are trying to edge someone off their presidential aspirations.

Kamala Harris has also admitted to having an affinity for songs by Tupac and Snoop Dogg. She said this on February 11th, 2019, on *The Breakfast Club*. It was in response to being asked by DJ Envy, a host on the morning show, what type of music she listens to and if Tupac and Snoop Dogg were among them. Again, another controversy was built around this reply. Charlamagne, another host of the same show had cut in before she could give Envy an answer. He wanted to know which songs Kamala listened to when she 'inhaled' in college (Kamala had also admitted to smoking marijuana while in school), but the

Senator laughed off the questions and when Envy asked, "Was it Snoop?" she replied to him instead.

The controversy here was that, since neither Tupac nor Snoop had released an album while Kamala was in college, she was simply telling lies in order to appeal to the black community in America. They conveniently overlooked the context in which she gave her reply.

In 2017, for African-American Music Appreciation Month, Kamala Harris shared her Spotify playlist which contained some of her favorite songs and musicians with Blavity, a website owned by Morgan DeBaun and that is targeted at 'Black Millennials'. It contained 45 songs, and included works by Tupac, Biggie, A Tribe Called Quest, Migos, John Legend, Childish Gambino, and others. The playlist was praised for its diversity and consistency with all she had said and written about her love for music.

Hobbies

By now, we already know that music was very much a part of Kamala's life as she was growing up, and that she continues to enjoy a good variety of songs even now. But did you know that the senator also loves to spend time in the kitchen? Her passion for cooking was ignited by her mother, who she described as a scientist even while cooking. According to Kamala, her mother loved to experiment with different ingredients in order to create new delicacies or give old ones a fresh taste. She would often join her mother in the kitchen, where Shyamala taught her various Indian recipes.

These days, Kamala likes to collect cookbooks. She has gathered quite a number of them and loves to relax with one in her hands. And this is when she's too tired to do any cooking. Besides the relaxing effect she gets from cooking or reading recipe books, she also says that preparing meals makes her feel normal. After a hectic week, there really is nothing like whipping up something delicious for family dinner on Saturdays to make a senator and aspiring president feel like a wife, mother, aunt, and daughter. Kamala's day can get so busy that she sometimes feels like she's not in control of her personal life. Cooking, especially for her family, is one activity that puts her in the mindset where she actually feels she's in control again (Silman, 2018). She also tries to cook with the tastes of those who are eating the food in mind. Ella, her stepdaughter, eats fish but avoids any meal with meat in it. As such, Kamala experiments with recipes that may include fish but have nothing to do with meat. Music also finds its way into the kitchen while she works her cooking magic.

When she can find the time, Kamala likes to go on vacation to two countries, besides America, that hold a warm place in her heart. She often visits India and Jamaica with her sister and niece. While there, they spend time with relatives in these countries and try the local delicacies.

Books

Kamala published two books in 2019. The first was her memoir, *The Truths We Hold*, which was published by Penguin Press and went on to become a bestseller. It received, on average, a 4 out of 5 rating by critics on Amazon. The second was a 40-page children's picture book called *Superheroes Are Everywhere*. It was published by Penguin Young Readers Group and has now gone up to the number 1 spot on the New York Times Bestsellers list. It was given a 4 out of 5 rating on Common Sense Media and has enjoyed similarly positive reviews from other sources. *Smart On Crime* was published in 2009 by Chronicle Books. It received fairly positive reviews, gaining 3.7 and 4.0 on Goodreads and Amazon respectively.

Income

On April 14th, 2019, Kamala Harris and her husband, Douglas Emhoff, declared a 2018 joint income of about $1.89 million. She also showed 15 years of tax returns, placing her among the presidential candidates to have released the most tax returns. By so doing, she has displayed a rare level of transparency and respect for the American populace. Her total income for the year 2018 was about $477,477. A large percentage of this figure are proceeds from *The Truths We Hold*, which was published in January of 2019, and quickly rose to become a bestseller. It amounted to $320,125. While the rest are from her salary as a Senator, which is a total of $157,352. Emhoff's income as a partner at DLA Piper law firm was about $1.3 million in 2018. Kamala and her husband paid taxes of up to $697,000 and gave about $27,259 as charity donations.

CHAPTER 5

OTHER KAMALA HARRIS
FACTS TO REMEMBER

1. Kamala Harris and her niece, Meena Harris, celebrate their birthdays on the same day: both of them were born on the 20th of October. Like Kamala, Meena is also a licensed lawyer.

2. Currently, Kamala is serving the United States of America as a junior Senator. She won the seat on the 8th of November, 2016, by defeating Loretta Sanchez and taking over from Barbara Boxer, who had decided to retire. She is the first person of either Jamaican or Indian roots to represent California in the Senate. She is also the third female Senator from California.

3. Although Kamala won by a narrow margin to become California's 32nd Attorney General in 2010 (she won by 46.1%, while Steve Cooley was only able to get 45.3% of the votes), her reelection in 2014 was a clean sweep. She beat her opponent, Ronald Gold, by claiming 57.5% of the votes to his 42.5%.

4. She challenged her then-boss, Terence Halinan, for the position of San Francisco District Attorney in 2003. She had ideas to fix the city and saw a problem with a scandalous personality like Terence being the D.A. In her words, she was "disillusioned and disappointed." Even though the odds were, seemingly, against her —she was a newcomer to politics— Kamala would press on and, eventually, clinch the win. She became the first ever female African-American District Attorney in the city of San Francisco.

5. Although Kamala admired her parents for being activists, she did not hope to be one herself. She dreamed of a more active role, where she did not have to protest, beg, or explain her objectives to anyone before doing what needed to be done. This was because she grew up to learn that many of the pleas and shouts by activists went unanswered. The way she saw it, she wanted the power to influence change from within, instead of banging the door helplessly from outside.

6. Senator Harris was a member of the Alpha Kappa Alpha sorority while attending Howard University. It was in college that she began to test the waters of politics. First, she majored in political science, giving her a more firm handle on what makes the world of politics tick. Then she campaigned to represent her freshman class in the Liberal Arts Student Council. She won.

7. Kamala was the name given to Senator Harris by her mother. The name has dual meaning in Hindu. It is used in reference to the Indian goddess of good fortune, Lakshmi, but could also mean lotus. The lotus is a flower that is used to symbolize purity, beauty, wisdom, prosperity, and spiritual enlightenment.

8. During her tenure as the District Attorney in San Francisco, Kamala Harris formed a unit whose focus was on hate crimes targeted at the LGBT community. She was especially interested in defending the rights of LGBT children and teenagers.

9. Between 2004 and 2007, she was honored with numerous prestigious awards. She was presented with the Child Advocate of the Year award by San Francisco Child Abuse Prevention Council in 2004. That same year, the National Urban League, a popular civil rights organization, recognized her as a Woman of Power. In 2005, the National Black Prosecutors Association gave her the Thurgood Marshall award. This award was named after the first African-American Supreme Court Justice who is respectfully remembered for the unparalleled and positively impactful role he played in the fight for equal opportunities for blacks and whites in America, Thurgood Marshall. Howard University recognized Kamala Harris as its Most Distinguished Alumni in 2006. Then, in 2007, Ebony magazine named her among the 100 Most Influential Black Americans.

10. Before September of 2011, many homeowners in California were swimming against the tumultuous waves of foreclosure threats. Kamala did what anyone raised under the wings of Shyamala Gopalan would have done: put her feet firmly down, and did the right thing, even though it was against popular opinion. Among the provisions in the Homeowner Bill of Rights is a ban against kickbacks by mortgage brokers, and borrowers are now allowed to sue mortgage lenders who attempt to skirt the law. This innovative bill was initiated and pushed for by then-Attorney General Kamala Harris. Yes, like her mom, she may have punched above her weight, but it paid off eventually.

11. In December, 2012, after warning Delta Airlines in advance (30 days, to be precise), Kamala Harris sued the company for refusing to comply with the laid-down law in California that demanded privacy notices in mobile applications. While she was not hesitant to praise the innovative tech culture that was booming in California, she also encouraged companies with mobile apps to respect the privacy of those people who use their apps. These tech companies were also urged to allow their users the choice of which information they would be comfortable with sharing.

12. Kamala Harris is often credited with being the first person to use the term "Muslim ban" in connection with President Donald Trump's order to stop Muslim refugees from seeking

asylum in the United States. In her statement, she begins by saying, "Make no mistake, this is a Muslim ban" (Harris, 2017). She explained that those Muslims running to America for safety may become tools in the hands of terrorists if they are rejected. In closing her speech, she said that refugees do not make America any less safe, instead they add to the economy.

13. In October of 2018, Kamala Harris, along with several other Democrats, was a target of a mail bomb. Had the package gotten to Kamala, it may have ended tragically. But the mail was intercepted by an employee at a postal service facility, who got suspicious and called the attention of the authorities. The mail was sent to Kamala's district office in Sacramento, and is believed to have been the doings of Cesar Sayoc. Mr. Sayoc is a man from Florida who tried to get rid of those who were critical of President Trump's leadership. His fingerprint was found on one of the crude explosive devices, and he later pleaded guilty to being responsible for the failed attacks.

14. Kamala Harris was among those who interrogated Mark Zuckerberg, founder and CEO of Facebook, about the misuse of private information belonging to users of the social network site. What pleased most people who watched the hearing was how Senator Kamala asked many of the questions they were hoping to ask themselves. Zuckerberg, who seemed poised and ready with well-rehearsed responses, quickly lost his composure and seemed between a rock and a hard place. This was because

he had no answers to justify the questions thrown at him. In the end, he appeared genuinely sorry.

15. Ironically, the fact above did not stop Kamala from using Facebook, which is still one of the best ways for a person to reach a large audience and get their point across. In 2018, Kamala apparently spent more money advertising through Facebook than all the other American senators.

16. Kamala's only sibling, Maya Harris, is a political analyst on the popular news channel, MSNBC, and used to be a policy advisor to Hillary Clinton during her presidential campaign. Maya's husband works for Uber as their General Counsel, and used to occupy the same position at PepsiCo. He was also an Associate Attorney General for the United States from 2012 to 2014.

17. Kamala Harris, during her tenure as D.A. in California, supported the matching of DNA results with family members of criminals, even when a direct match cannot be made. Often, certain cases are forgotten because the authorities could not match the DNA to any suspects. This may be because the DNA of the criminal is not in the database of the police and other relevant security agencies. As such, it is more effective to compare DNA with familial matches. They have even gone further to compare their samples with those on genealogy websites.

18. In 2012, Kamala Harris did what most people would not have the guts to see through. An illegal immigrant, Sergio Garcia, was applying for a law license. He had arrived with his parents in the United States more than 20 years prior from Mexico as a child, but still had not been nationalized. More than his green card, what worried Sergio the most was his license to practice law in California. Kamala Harris got wind of his predicament and submitted a brief in support of Sergio. In 2014, the California Supreme Court ruled in favor of Sergio, deeming him worthy to practice as a lawyer regardless of his status. He had met all the requirements necessary for a law license and his only unlawful act for more than 2 decades in America was illegally staying in the country.

19. Among the first things she said upon becoming a Senator was that, even though an undocumented immigrant is in violation of civil law, the individual could not be considered a criminal. Entering the United States without permission, after getting deported, is a crime. But running from murder capitals in search of asylum in America is not.

20. In 2017, Kamala displayed her extraordinary courage again. She refused to vote for an end of the year spending bill until the DACA issue was addressed. Deferred Action for Childhood Arrivals (DACA) is a program for individuals whose parents brought them illegally into the country when they were little children. If such a child grows up to be law abiding, a good

student, and productive member of the society, then they are to be protected from deportation. As at October, 2017, the Senate was going to sign a spending bill without resolving this crucial issue. Kamala would have none of it, and she stood by her convictions.

21. Kamala Harris is the first Indian-American woman to become a Senator in the United States.

22. Kamala Harris continues to stand her ground on rejecting the death penalty as a crime deterrent. But this ground has been rocked many times, and may happen again in the future. In 2004, an on-duty cop, Officer Isaac Espinoza, was shot and killed by a gang member. Although a sizeable percentage of the population in San Francisco were against the death penalty, many in that city expected her to do the obvious: have the killer sentenced to death. But she didn't do that. Instead, David Hill was given his day in court and sentenced to life in prison without the possibility of parole. Many were enraged by her choice, especially the family of Officer Espinoza and cops around the city. But she has had some success in rebuilding her relationship with the police force and continues to maintain her stance on the death penalty as being mostly ineffective at controlling crime.

23. Chicken masala and korma are Senator Harris's favorite Indian delicacies. Her Indian restaurants of choice are Dosa and Amber India.

24. Kamala is of the belief that working out and cooking are the best ways to relax. Another thing she loves to do is make routines, and Kamala has made working out in the morning a part of her daily routine.

25. As Attorney General, a page was set up on the office's website that went into detail about the laws concerning cyber exploitation. She made it clear that sexual offenses through the internet would be prosecuted, and those found guilty may even face jail time.

26. Harris sometimes describes herself, during her time as District Attorney, as a vigilante. She was so concerned about the rate at which people below the age of 25 were getting killed and how it was connected to inconsistent class attendance and dropping out of high school, that she felt she had to do something about it. She created a system where parents were pressured to ensure their kids were not involved in any kind of truancy. Parents were even faced with being prosecuted to this effect.

CONCLUSION

Kamala Harris exemplifies the strength, courage, and defiant will of a woman of conviction as she continues to explore her potential on the road to fulfilling her dreams. She has lived up to her name, as like the lotus, her compassion, fairness, and grace shine ever so brightly despite the muddy waters of the political world she has to tread through. While she is not without her faults and flaws, her determination to not be distracted, to keep an open mind, and to continue to reevaluate her choices are what make her stand out as a person of character.

Made in the USA
Middletown, DE
22 August 2024

59563372R00027